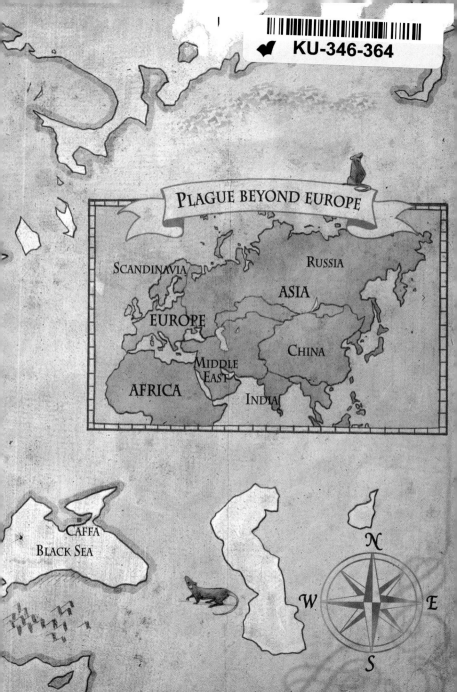

KU-346-364

PLAGUE BEYOND EUROPE

SCANDINAVIA

RUSSIA

ASIA

EUROPE

CHINA

MIDDLE
EAST

AFRICA

INDIA

CAFFA

BLACK SEA

N

W

E

S

The Black Death

Rob Lloyd Jones
Illustrated by Daniele Dickmann

Reading consultant: Alison Kelly

Contents

Chapter 1

Dark news

A fat black rat scurried down a gangplank, as sailors unloaded ships at a dock at Messina, Sicily.

It was October 1347, and the ships had just arrived from the Black Sea, loaded with sacks of spices. They had also brought dark news…

"Something terrible is happening in the Saracen lands," a sailor reported. "Some sort of sickness, a plague, is killing thousands."

No one paid attention. The Saracens (the name given to Muslims) were a long way away. Besides, such stories weren't unusual. Diseases spread fast in dirty places, and at that time – the Middle Ages – most towns were dirty.

Although people tried to keep the streets clean, towns were often strewn with rubbish and rotten vegetable peel. This mixed with dung from cows, horses and pigs, and waste from fishmongers, slaughterhouses and taverns.

Dirty places attracted rats, and rats carried fleas. The sailors in Messina didn't know it, but the plague in Asia had been spread by fleas that lived on black rats. When a flea bit a human, the disease got into the person's blood.

Nor did the sailors know that they had carried infected fleas with them, on rats that stowed away on their ships.

The plague had already killed 25 million people, from southern Russia – where it probably began – to China, India and North Africa.

Now the sailors had brought it to Europe. The world would never be the same again.

Chapter 2

Signs of sickness

"Lord have mercy on us!" The cry rang out across Marseilles, France, as another victim of the plague collapsed in the street. No one rushed to help. Everyone fled, leaving the corpse on the ground.

From Sicily, the plague had swept along the Mediterranean coast. It reached Marseilles in the winter of 1347, and killed half the city. At the same time, trade ships arriving at Italian ports brought more rats from Asia, and more infected fleas.

Traders spread the plague on foot, too. As they journeyed from town to town selling goods, they carried infected fleas in their clothing, and on rats that hid in their carts.

Everyone knew the signs of the plague. First, victims got a terrible headache and were sick. They coughed up blood and their muscles ached with cramps. Then they got a fever and became very tired.

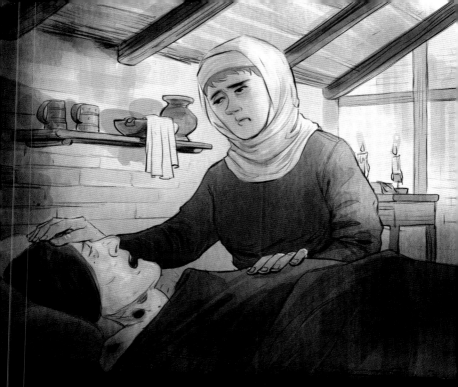

Dark, swollen lumps – known as *buboes* – grew on their necks, thighs and armpits.

Sometimes plague victims died in just two days. Sometimes they suffered for a week. But they almost always died. Very few people recovered.

In fact, not all victims had the *same* plague. There were different forms of the disease, which struck in different ways.

One plague infected victims' lungs and was spread by coughs and sneezes. Another attacked people's blood.

The most common type of the disease was 'bubonic' plague. It left victims dotted with the dark buboes that later gave this outbreak of the plague its nickname – the Black Death.

By January 1348, the Black
Death had spread north to Italy.
In Venice, boatmen steered barges
along the canals, calling out,
"Corpi morti! Corpi morti! Dead bodies!
Dead bodies!" Corpses were dropped
from doorways, and onto a pile
on the boats.

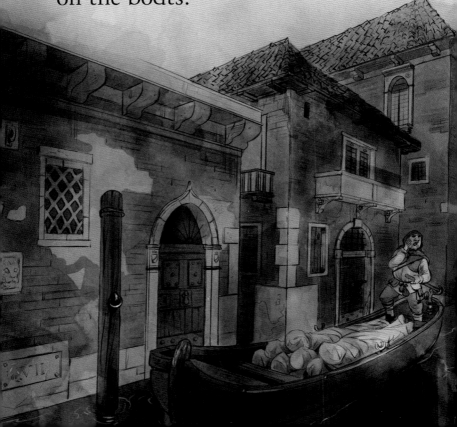

In Siena, shoemaker Agnolo di Tura watched the nightmare scenes and wrote, "This is the end of the world."

To most people that was exactly how it seemed.

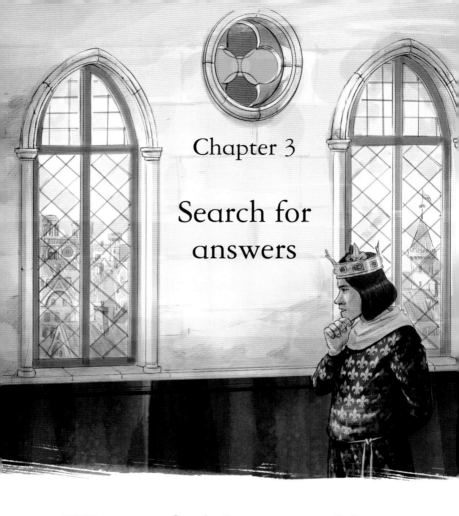

Chapter 3

Search for answers

"We must find the cause of this plague!" declared King Philip VI of France, in October 1348. "Until we know its cause, we cannot stop it."

The Black Death had reached Paris in June that year. As it spread around the crowded streets, it killed around 100,000 people, halving the city's population.

Scholars from the University of Paris gathered to investigate. They studied medical texts and maps of the stars, and then blamed earthquakes and the position of the planets for the spread of the disease.

The truth was, no one had a clue. But everyone wanted an answer, a way to explain all the deaths.

Some thought the plague was carried in bad air, caused by the filthy conditions of their towns. But to most people the reason for the plague was clear: it was a punishment from God for their sins.

A group known as the 'flagellants' were desperate for God to forgive them. Dressed in white, gangs paraded through villages in central Europe, singing hymns and lashing themselves viciously with whips.

Villagers surrounded them, joining hands and singing, "Save us! Save us!"

As they journeyed through
Europe, the flagellants spread
a terrible lie. They claimed that
people of the Jewish faith had
deliberately caused the plague
by poisoning wells. Furious mobs
attacked Jewish communities.

In the city of Strasbourg (now in France), 2,000 Jews were burned at the stake by a bloodthirsty mob.

In Mainz, Germany, around 6,000 Jews were dragged from their homes and killed.

The murders didn't stop at Jews. Anyone who seemed different was blamed. Beggars and even pilgrims became targets of people's rage. Anyone with any sign of illness could be murdered.

Everyone thought they knew how the plague was spreading, but no one really did. And so no one could stop it.

Chapter 4

No mercy

From France, the plague spread
to Spain and then Portugal.
It reached England by June,
1348, and by the end of that year,
200 people a day were dying
in London. Carts
were pushed
around the
city to collect
the dead.

Dead bodies were taken outside the city and buried in long plague pits. In some, the dead were stacked five deep in neat rows.

In Wales, poet Jeuan Gethin wrote, "We see death coming into our midst like black smoke... a rootless phantom which has no mercy."

No one was safe. The Black Death killed rich and poor. It killed lords and ladies. It killed bishops and archbishops. It even killed royalty, when the daughter of Edward III, king of England, died of the plague in France.

More women and children were dying than men. They spent more time indoors, in cramped cottages where plague spread fast.

More poor people died than rich, whose stone houses were harder for rats to invade than peasants' cottages. Fewer rats meant fewer infected fleas.

Desperate, people tried to protect
themselves by pressing bunches of
herbs over their mouth and nose.
They hoped this would stop them
from breathing 'bad air'.

Some people believed that fire would 'clean' the infected air. In Rome, Pope Clement VI sat inside a circle of crackling fire torches. In fact, fire did work against the plague, because it drove away fleas.

In some towns, church bells rang throughout the day, because loud noises were thought to drive infection from the air.

Doctors had no idea how to stop the plague either, though they tried all sorts of cures.

They pierced victims' skin to let 'infected blood' run out...

...they washed people in vinegar, urine, and rose water...

...and made potions from herbs, tree resin, flowers and roots.

The only real way to escape the plague was to run. When the disease struck, people fled to the safety of an uninfected area. Often those who ran already had the plague, or carried fleas in their clothes and carts.

So the Black Death continued to spread.

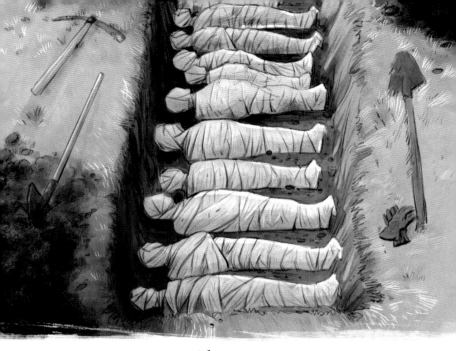

Chapter 5

Desperate days

By 1349, the Black Death was claiming around 7,500 lives a day as it spread around Europe. It seemed as if it wouldn't stop until every single person was dead.

People wrote wills, expecting to die. Roads were often crammed with people fleeing infected towns. Inns and taverns closed. Farms were abandoned and crops withered in the fields.

Still the plague kept spreading. From England, the crew of a wool ship carried it to Scandinavia. In 1350, King Magnus II of Sweden declared, "God, for the sins of men, has struck the world with this great punishment…"

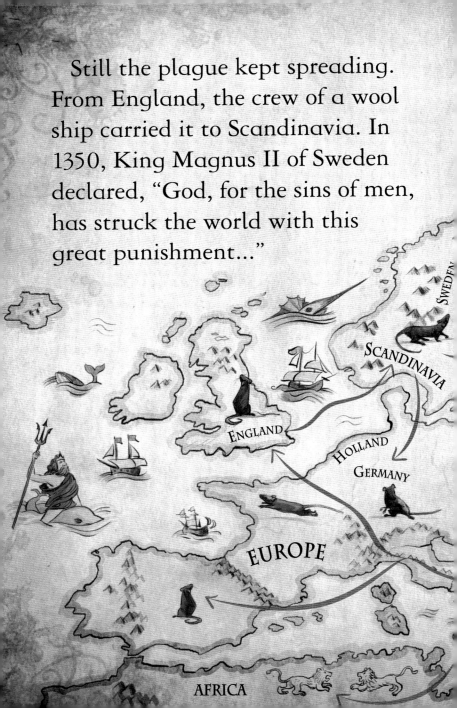

SWEDEN

SCANDINAVIA

ENGLAND

HOLLAND

GERMANY

EUROPE

AFRICA

It spread to Holland, where church bells rang for two days in warning. It spread to Germany. It spread to western Russia. Hardly anywhere in Europe was spared.

RUSSIA

CAFFA

ASIA

Fear spread as fast as the disease. Doctors started refusing to treat the sick, scared of catching the plague themselves. Priests stopped praying with victims.

People began to take desperate measures to stop the Black Death reaching their town. Town gates were shut to outsiders. Traders who had visited plague-infected places were banned from coming home.

Ships were searched at docks.
If corpses were found on board, the
ship was burned and the crew was
thrown out of town. Other ships
weren't even allowed to dock.
They drifted at sea until their
whole crew was dead.

Among the panic there were acts
of kindness too. In a Paris hospital,
nuns remained with victims. If a
nun caught the plague and died,
another took her place.

In Perugia, one of Italy's most famous doctors, Gentile da Foligno, stayed among the sick until he was killed by the plague as well.

Most people, though, wanted nothing whatsoever to do with plague victims.

Chapter 6

Life after death

By 1353, more and more towns were trying to stop the disease from spreading. People stayed away from infected places and kept their homes and streets cleaner. Finally, the Black Death began to die down.

GREENLAND

SCANDINAVIA

EUROPE
HALF OF THE POPULATION
DEAD – AROUND 25 MILLION

ATLANTIC OCEAN

NORTH
AFRICA

THE MIDDLE EAST
AROUND A THIRD OF
THE POPULATION KILLED

How many people had died? It's hard to say. In most places no one kept a record, while in others people exaggerated the number of deaths.

The plague killed around 25 million people in China and India. In Europe, between 1347 and 1353, around the same number died

ASIA
AT LEAST 25
MILLION DEAD

CHINA

INDIA

   The plague also spread west to
Greenland, south to North Africa,
and ravaged the Middle East. In
total, the Black Death killed at
least 100 million people. There
may even have been as many as
200 million victims, which was
half of the world at that time.

The world was a different place after the Black Death. Some villages were left totally empty. In others, people had to move away in search of work, so those villages were eventually deserted, too.

Since there were fewer people
to do the work, farm workers
demanded more money and better
rights. Craftsmen were able to
charge higher prices for their goods.

Many people began to have
more control over their lives
than they had before the plague.

Rich people panicked. They wanted society to stay the same, with them at the top and peasants at the bottom. In England, a law was passed to stop peasants from earning more money than they had before the Black Death.

Anger at the new law led to a revolt.

In June 1381, an angry mob of peasants marched over London Bridge, captured the Tower of London and chopped off an archbishop's head. But after their leader, Wat Tyler, was killed, most of the peasants simply trudged back home.

Chapter 7

Plague returns

The Black Death lasted seven years, but plagues ravaged Europe for the next three centuries. More and more, though, people acted to stop disease from spreading to other towns. So, when plague came back, it only hit particular places.

But it still hit them *hard*.

In 1466, plague killed 40,000 people in Paris. In 1649, an even worse outbreak left over 60,000 people dead in Seville, Spain. Rows of bodies were left in the city's streets, to be collected by carts.

London was ravaged by the disease for seven terrible months in 1665, an outbreak now known as the 'Great Plague'. Victims were locked in their homes, and red crosses were painted as warnings on the doors. Below the cross were scrawled the words 'Lord have mercy upon us.'

Those doctors brave enough to treat victims wore special costumes to protect themselves — leather hats and gowns, as well as a mask with a long 'beak' stuffed with herbs to purify the air the doctors breathed.

Still, people didn't know what caused the plague. In London, cats were blamed and rounded up and killed.

In fact, cats were useful during a plague. They killed rats, which really *were* spreading the disease. So in London things got even worse.

The plague came back again in Asia in the middle of the 1800s, killing around 12 million people in China and India.

It struck India again in 1994, although far fewer people died. It even still exists today. Every year there are a few cases in parts of Asia and North America.

We know a lot about the plague thanks to its victims. Workers clearing land for new buildings sometimes dig up medieval plague pits. Archaeologists then study the site and remains to find out more about the Black Death.

Scientists have even found traces of the disease in the victims' bones. These traces revealed what the plague was and how it spread, and also helped them develop a cure.

Even so, there are things we *don't* know about the Black Death, such as where exactly it began. Over 650 years after it first struck, we still have a lot to learn about a tragedy that changed the world forever.

Timeline of the Black Death

1338

First reports
of a plague in
Central Asia

By 1347

The Black Death has killed around
25 million people in Asia, from
southern Russia to China and India.

October 1348

King Philip VI of France gathers scholars
to investigate the causes of the disease.

February 1349

Around 2,000 Jews
are murdered in
Strasbourg...

August 1349

...and around 6,000
in Mainz, Germany.

1466

Plague kills 40,000
people in Paris.

June 1381

'The Peasants
Revolt' in London

1649

An outbreak leaves
over 60,000 people
dead in Seville, Spain.

1665

The 'Great Plague' in
London kills half the city.

October 1347

The plague reaches Messina, Sicily.

January 1348

Half of Florence, Italy, is killed by the disease.

June 1348

It spreads to Spain and Portugal, and to England.

The Black Death kills 100,000 in Paris, France.

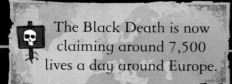

The Black Death is now claiming around 7,500 lives a day around Europe.

1350

The disease reaches Sweden and Denmark.

1353

The Black Death finally seems to be over.

1351

It reaches western Russia.

1877-1889

An outbreak of plague kills 12 million people in China and India.

1994

Plague kills 54 people in India.

Usborne Quicklinks

For links to websites to find out more about the
Black Death, go to the Usborne Quicklinks
website at **www.usborne.com/quicklinks** and
type in the title of this book.
Please follow the internet safety guidelines
at the Usborne Quicklinks website.
Usborne Publishing cannot be responsible
for any website other than its own.

Designed by Samantha Barrett
Series editor: Lesley Sims
Series designer: Russell Punter
Digital manipulation by John Russell
Historical consultant: Dr. Anne Millard

First published in 2018 by Usborne Publishing Ltd.,
Usborne House, 83-85 Saffron Hill, London EC1N 8RT, England.
www.usborne.com Copyright © 2018 Usborne Publishing Ltd.

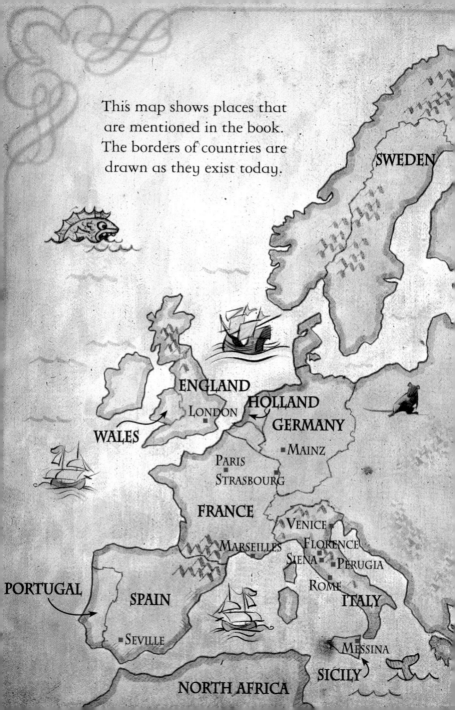

This map shows places that are mentioned in the book. The borders of countries are drawn as they exist today.

SWEDEN

ENGLAND
LONDON
HOLLAND
GERMANY
WALES
MAINZ
PARIS
STRASBOURG
FRANCE
VENICE
MARSEILLES
FLORENCE
SIENA
PERUGIA
ROME
ITALY
PORTUGAL
SPAIN
SEVILLE
MESSINA
SICILY
NORTH AFRICA